The Apple

A play by Jack Gelber

The Apple

Grove Press, Inc.
New York

Library of Congress Catalog Card Number: 61-10904

First Printing 1961

Manufactured in the United States of America

FOR

THE LIVING THEATRE

The Performers:

THE APPLE was first performed on November 28, 1961 at the Living Theatre, New York City, directed by Judith Malina with the following cast:

ACE	*A Negro*	James Earl Jones
JABEZ	*A Con Man* . . .	John Coe
ANNA	*An Oriental-American*	Marion Jim
AJAX	*A Nihilist*	Julian Beck
MR. STARK	*A Spastic*	Henry Proach
IRIS	*A Hustler*	Cynthia Robinson
TOM	*A former Silent Screen Actor* . .	Fred Miller

NOTE: In production all the actors should use their own names.

Act One

In the lobby before the play begins drunken TOM *offers several members of the audience a drink from his pint bottle. He accuses them of pushing him around and makes a paranoid nuisance of himself.*

No curtain. A restaurant or coffee shop. ANNA, JABEZ *and* ACE *are serving drinks to the audience. A radio is playing.* ANNA *turns it off.*

ACE:

Sorry, no more drinks. Show about to begin.

(ANNA *and* JABEZ *exit.*)

Okay! Okay! Let's everyone take a seat and do something right for a change. You, you over there, be a good fellow and sit down. Let's all take a deep breath.

(*Takes a deep breath*)

And let's start off alive. It's getting near opening time and a few words are necessary as we are not all here. Up here or down there, in here or out there we are not all here. Apparently we are all seated. Yes. Good. Now, did everyone take a breath of air? I don't want a dead crew right from the jump. Breath creates. Yes sir and madam, I'll say it again: breath creates. If you don't believe me, try not breathing. When you breathe your muscles move and when your body is moving you get to feel good and warm all over. You keep moving, baby, because that's being alive. Alive. Don't look now but they can arrest you for that. Okay! Okay! We're together.

We're all here.

(ANNA *enters with bowl of apples.*)

Let's have a ball. Which brings me to the point—I don't want you to despair. You're going to witness and may be part of some destructive scenes. That might take over your mind and make you forget just how warm your body is. Don't let it happen. Don't despair. Smile. This is no joking matter. We are going to eat up the set, the audience, and nibble a little on ourselves. Don't get too smart now—a little knowledge is small potatoes. For you economic necessity may be a thing of the past, but it will drive some way out, way out. People call me a fakir. Some call me a brilliant man. It doesn't matter. Call me a snake charmer or a paramour, it all comes out the same. Out, man, that's a cue, you heard me, it all comes out the same.

(*Lights out.* ACE *exits. Lights up. Enter* JABEZ *carrying a mannequin.*)

JABEZ:

Look what Ajax left backstage. We can really use this!

ANNA:

Where is he?

JABEZ:

He's late. We'll just have to exploit that fact.
(*Begins to fling paint on glass*)
I heard that! Don't think I can't hear you. Yes, leave

your name at the box office. We see applicants every day.

ANNA:

I'm in charge tonight. I don't kid. Leave your name at the box office and the entire cast will interview you.

JABEZ:

We vote you in or we vote you out. Very democratic. I know what you're thinking. I'll admit why I'm here—therapy. That's not the only reason for being here. Make up your own reason.

ANNA:

We have an impressive list of graduates.

JABEZ:

We embrace all schools of acting! Except the closet school. Precision! That's what we aim for—precision! Naturally it doesn't always come out that way. Art is precision. Control, control every gesture, every word. Everything depends on the plan, the design. Anna, did you hear that? That man said he didn't have to pay to get in here. I work on a percentage. You can't give away free seats. Except for the critics, except for the critics.

ANNA:

Oh, shut up, Jabez! I'm not giving anything away. Say, that's a pretty painting!

JABEZ:

I knew I could count on that. It's something to hold on to. Do you like it?

ANNA:

Ace, will you bring us something to drink?

ACE:

(*From backstage*)

Out. Out. Out.

(*His voice chants from a speaker at the rear of the theatre.*

Out. Out. Out. I'll be right out.

ANNA:

(*To audience*)

Why is it that everyone is on time every night, except when I'm in charge? Where's Iris?

JABEZ:

You know Iris.

ANNA:

It's like the solar system. Stars revolving around a sun. Never touching, never touching.

JABEZ:

That's touching.

ANNA:

(*Moving and talking to mannequin*)

Yeah. Well, I'm old enough to know when someone is paying attention to me. Can we have a play where our configuration is like the structure of a nucleus. everyone pays attention to each other? You know

(ACE *enters.*)

Celestial and indifferent to one another.

ACE:

(*To* JABEZ)

Are you indulging again?

(*To* ANNA)

Here you are, baby.

ANNA:

Don't baby me.

ACE:

That's just my way of telling you that I know what's happening.

ANNA:

You know everything and nothing.

JABEZ:

Someone save us. We're in for a mystical evening.

ACE:

(*To* ANNA)

Don't despair. They'll show up—separately.

ANNA:

That's right. Reduce it all to the immediate common-place.

JABEZ:

Here we go again. The wheel of life is spinning and

where she stops is over the moon and beyond this hovel we call living. Half the fun is not betting.

ACE:

Nothing up this sleeve. And nothing up this one. Relax. There isn't any grand design.

JABEZ:

No design is a grand design.

(*Enter* AJAX *with sunglasses: one glass is missing. He is helping a spastic to a table.*)

AJAX:

Hello, everybody. Sorry I'm late. Better late than never, eh? I've brought my replacement.

(*Helps the spastic take off his coat and at the same time tries to kiss* ANNA)

JABEZ:

I didn't vote.

ANNA:

What do you mean? You can't leave now.

STARK:

(*Grunts*)

AJAX:

Oh, baby, the pressure must be fantastic. Don't worry, my replacement is just about the funniest man in the universe.

(*To* JABEZ' *painting*)

Whose wet dream it that?

Mr. Stark, meet Anna, Jabez and Ace.

STARK:

(*Grunts*)

ANNA:

You're mean and despicable. You can't leave me tonight.

AJAX:

All right, so I'll stick around and help break in my replacement.

JABEZ:

I didn't vote for him. Is he from Real Life Drama?

ANNA:

Get rid of him! Get rid of him!

AJAX:

We can't throw him out in the street like some unwanted cat. I went to great lengths to steal him from a Boy Scout who was taking him across the street. Besides, do you realize Mr. Stark is the most intelligent former mayor of Cicero, Illinois? We have a celebrity. I mean the man can speak Etruscan.

STARK:

(*Grunts*)

AJAX:

There you are. He's speaking Etruscan. I'll translate for you.

STARK:

(*Grunts*)

AJAX:

C.

STARK:

(*Grunts*)

AJAX:

H.

STARK:

(*Grunts*)

AJAX:

I.

STARK:

(*Grunts*)

AJAX:

N.

STARK:

(*Grunts*)

AJAX:

K.

ANNA:

You're terrible.

AJAX:

How about something to drink for my friend, Ace?

(*Enter* IRIS.)

IRIS:

Hi, everybody. I've just tried to sell my body.

JABEZ:

You bitch! Are you hustling again?

IRIS:

Oh, don't look so silly, Jabez. I mean for scientific purposes.

AJAX:

Anything for science, I always say.

IRIS:

Oh, no. No. I mean you sell your body to a university. They tattoo the address of the university on your body. When you die, no matter where you are, they ship your body to this university and they perform experiments on it, scientific ones. You get two hundred and fifty dollars.

ANNA:

You're late.

IRIS:

You aren't mad are you? I came by taxi. I met this man at the hospital that was going my way. I thought it was very neighborly . . .

JABEZ:

Did you get the money for your body?

IRIS:

It's all a damn lie. Ajax, do you hear me, Mister Joker?

AJAX:

Iris, I'd like you to meet Mr. Stark.

IRIS:

How do you do?

(*Tries to shake* STARK's *hand*)

It's just like you. Just like you.

JABEZ:

What were you doing at a hospital?

IRIS:

Giving blood. Damn them! Last year they were giving twenty-five dollars for a pint of blood. Now the price is only ten bucks.

AJAX:

You can't trust anyone these days. Ace, we need a spoon to feed Mr. Stark.

STARK:

(*Grunts and flays arms*)

ACE:

I left them backstage.

JABEZ:

I'll get it. I'll get it.

(*Exits*)

ANNA:

(*Takes a bite of apple*)

You give that poor man of yours a very rough time. I'm beginning to be sorry I ever introduced you to each other.

(*Gives the apple to* IRIS *who takes a bite*)

IRIS:

Oh, don't be silly. Jabez likes me to be critical.

STARK:

(*Grunts*)

IRIS:

I'll bet he understands everything we say. I'll bet if he could talk, he could really say . . . well, anyway— how do we know what he knows? Do you see what I mean? How do we—

AJAX:

(*Takes apple from* IRIS)
The gentleman would like to dance.

ANNA:

Will you get rid of him?

JABEZ:

(*From rear speaker*)
You can't get rid of me that easily.

STARK:

(*Moans*)

JABEZ:

Time was when you pleaded with me to stay. I want to survive. So I keep my eye on the accounts. You resent it. Don't deny it. I'm not in the room but I can see you.

IRIS:

Jabez, will you stop playing with the toys backstage?

JABEZ:

That's what I love about you, dear. Yes, you say exactly the wrong thing at the right time. I want to play. That's what I go through every night. Who shall I be tonight?

STARK:

(*Moans*)

JABEZ:

What I wanted was simple enough. Start from the beginning. Do the Adam and Eve bullshit.

ACE:

Jabez, please bring out that spoon. This man is thirsting to beat hell.

JABEZ:

(*Enters*)

I just didn't have it tonight. I should have entranced the whole lot of you. I should have . . . I apologize.

(AJAX *spoon-feeds the drink to* STARK.)

ANNA:

The scene . . . would you darken the stage except for this table.

(*Points to the table where* AJAX *and* STARK *are seated*)

The scene is a dentist's office.

(*Puts on record of "Grand Canyon Suite"*)
Dr. Ajax is examining his first patient of the morning, Mr. Stark. His assistant is the lovely Miss Iris.

IRIS:

Oh, no!

ANNA:

Oh, yes.

IRIS:

I want to be the patient.

ANNA:

I suspected that! We don't always get what we want, do we, dear? In the waiting room we have a rich man, Mr. Ace, and a poor man, Mr. Jabez.

JABEZ:

Oh, God, another social commentary.

ACE:

Shut up, boy, or I'll take out my whip.

JABEZ:

(*Turns off music*)
It's so corny. I don't get anything out of it. If I can't get anything out of it why am I here? I ask you. Why am I here? Why?
(*Thinks he hears something in the audience*)
I will not leave. All right, I'll give a startling performance. I accept this challenge against my better judgment.

ANNA:

(*Puts music on*)
Shut up and let me go on.
(*Stops* JABEZ *from apologizing*)
Just keep still.

JABEZ:

My tooth hoits, lady. My tooth.

(ANNA *bows and steps to the side.*)

AJAX:

Did anyone ever tell you that you have interesting teeth?

STARK:

(*Grunts*)

AJAX:

Nurse, prepare for a class three gold foil.

IRIS:

Doctor, would you take a look at this?
(*Opens her mouth*)
It's just killing me.

AJAX:

Not now, dear. Just make the preparations.

IRIS:

Oh, why do the patients have all the fun?

(ANNA *puts the mannequin between* JABEZ *and* ACE *and retreats.*)

JABEZ:

(*To* ACE)

Is this a good dentist?

(*To mannequin*)

What's wrong with me? Why won't this guy talk to me? Ah, he probably came to have all his good teeth removed and gold ones put in. What are you here for?

AJAX:

Open a little wider. That's it!

(STARK *bites his finger.*)

Aaaah! You bastard!

ACE:

I can't stand pain. Obviously I have the wrong dentist.

(*Rises to leave*)

IRIS:

You can't leave us.

(*Grabs* ACE)

ACE:

Will you take those lovely white hands off of me!

AJAX:

Nurse! Nurse! Prepare for the injection.

(IRIS *takes an enormous hypodermic needle out of the mannequin's head.*)

ACE:

I'm afraid this will never do.

JABEZ:

No guts! You get a few bucks and all you want is security. How's the Doc going to save them pearly whites if you chicken out on him now?

ACE:

Will you never mention the word chicken in my presence.

(*Sits down. To mannequin*)

Would you mind telling me why you have no clothes on?

JABEZ:

That's the nicest thing you've said.

AJAX:

Now this isn't going to hurt one little bit. Just open wide.

(STARK *opens his mouth.*)

This reminds me of the time I had a chili pepper *aficionado* in the chair. He had just returned from a field trip on Avery Island in Louisiana. He burned out three class one silver fillings on the buckle side and one on the labial. Oh yes, what a mouth! The gold on his crown was eroded.

STARK:

(*Grunts*)

AJAX:

Just keep the mouth open, please. That's right. Come to think of it there was that fellow from the Philippines. Chewed betel nut. Just about the best case of decay and discoloration I've ever seen.

ACE:

Nice day out.

JABEZ:

Yeah.

ACE:

I'm here for a cleaning.

AJAX:

Have you tried brushing your teeth?

STARK:

(*Grunts*)

AJAX:

Just keep the mouth open, please.

(*Enter a drunk*, TOM, *from audience.*)

TOM:

Hey!

(*Beat*)

Hey!

ANNA:

Now what? Are you back again?

(*Turns music off*)

You're not wanted here.

TOM:

Hey!

AJAX:

Hey what?

TOM:

Hey, I want a drink. Have you been waiting for me?

AJAX:

Oh, I thought you were another Etruscan.

TOM:

Hey, I want to buy a beer.

JABEZ:

Money is money.

IRIS:

That's the guy who took me here in the taxi.

TOM:

Hi, kiddo. I was hoping I'd find you.

ACE:

This place is a restaurant. We don't serve liquor.

TOM:

Hey! Who is that, Joe Louis?

ACE:

I might turn into Joe and flatten your ass. You can't get away with *that!*

TOM:

Hey, let me buy you all a beer.

JABEZ:

I know you. What's your name? I know your face.

ANNA:

Ajax, will you get rid of him?

AJAX:

Apparently you think I'm an exterminator.

TOM:

Kill 'em! Kill 'em all!

JABEZ:

What's your name?

TOM:

Is this a quiz show?

(AJAX *takes* TOM*'s arm.*)

TOM:

I warn you! I've got a bad heart. I warn you.
Don't touch me.

IRIS:

I met him at the hospital.

(ACE *pushes* TOM *into a seat.*)

STARK:

(*Grunts*)

TOM:

I'm a radio. You know what I mean? I'm a goddamn radio. I receive messages all the time.
(*Points to* STARK)
He's a radio, too. It takes one to know one.
(*Imitates radio static*)

STARK:

(Grunts)

TOM:

I got your message. I got your message.
(Lays his head on the table and goes to sleep)

IRIS:

He looks dead to me.

ANNA:

Quit being a child.

ACE:

I vote no. I can't make any J. Louis scene. Later.
(Exits)

AJAX:

Sensitive, isn't he?
(Lifts STARK *up. Begins a dance with him.)*
I wish I knew how to dance. How long has it been since you've danced, Mr. Stark? I usually dance alone. It's nice to have the company. Two, three, four. You know what I like about you, Mr. Stark? You can tell your story without a word.

STARK:

(Grunts)

IRIS:

He's in pain.

AJAX:

No false empathy, please. What was that, Mr. Stark?

STARK:

(*Grunts*)

AJAX:

How dare you, sir! I am not participating in any sex orgy. The very idea of it! No, Mr. Stark, I'm very disappointed. No, you can't take your clothes off. Absolutely not!

ANNA:

Stop it!

AJAX:

Don't be jealous, dear. I'll dance with you next.

ANNA:

(*Mimes fixing a tie on the mannequin. Near the end of the following she begins her dance with it.*)

Oh shit! Always the seductress!

(*To mannequin*)

You lead. I'll follow. I'm always following. That's right: if you were a scientist, I'd learn about bugs. What do they care? Open your mouth and exhale some bugs on them and they say, "What a crazy chick!" or "Blow, baby, blow!"

ACE:

(*From the rear speaker*)

We're rolling. We're getting there. The theatre is an enormous eye. The audience is the eyeball. The light from the outside comes through the eyeball and focuses on the stage. I got the whole thing worked out. The cornea, the vitreous humor, the retina, the center of the blind spot—I got it all worked out. But why get technical? Oh, it would be all right if everyone were an oculist. But you get my meaning.

(ANNA *pulls off one of the mannequin's arms and gives it to* IRIS. JABEZ *begins painting.*)

STARK:

(*Groans*)

ACE:

Thank you. Thank you. Any sound will do it. Because I want to say hearing is talking. Mr Stark grunts and he's saying something. He's talking to you. What you pick up—that's what's important. You hear it, you get behind it and then it talks to you.

(IRIS *nonchalantly sings a wordless song under the following.*)

ACE:

After all, we got to start somewhere. Let's go back to the beginning.

ANNA:

We relive it every night.

(*Stops dancing.* IRIS *tries to put the mannequin arm on the body.*)

ACE:

We've got a long time before we get everyone working behind the senses. Look at this! Two people meeting on the street. Every gesture, every sound is singing. What a brotherhood! I'll work for that kind of universe.

AJAX:

All goeth out. All returneth within. There shall be an end of ends.

(*Stops dancing. Singing ends. A long pause.*)

TOM:

(*Stands up more or less sober*)

I'm with a bunch of goddamned intellectuals! Hey! Have a drink!

(*Offers his pint bottle*)

You talk about life where there is no life. I can't stand you! What do you know about comedy? Nothing.

AJAX:

Why don't you leave?

TOM:

I can't leave now. Have a drink? Why do all minorities love the spiritual? Ugh! What a somber crowd this is!

JABEZ:

It's so sad. Iris, Iris, sing again.

TOM:

Iris sweetie, the Jewboy wants you to warble.

IRIS:

Why . . .

JABEZ:

He's not well, Iris. Don't botter with him. What is your name?

TOM:

Your humility is disgusting. Have a drink. I don't mean any harm. I talk too much. But, goddamn it, do you have to bring up this New York bull. Next thing I know you'll ask me, "And what do you do?" You people never lose control. You don't ever get drunk, so what good are you? You think you know all about the spirit that moves you. Well, I'm spiritual, too. Kill, kill, kill. Kill the Jews, niggers, obliterate the slants, let's see, who else is here, oh yes, that spastic must go. Sonofabitch, you are a bunch of torture freaks. Where's Mister Bones, I want a beer chaser.

AJAX:

(*Imitating* TOM's *gestures*)

No one loves me. Oh, oh, oh.

(*Darts to* TOM *and kisses him on the forehead, retreats*)

TOM:

Get away from me you goddamn ballet dancer.

JABEZ:

All right, I'll do something about it. I volunteer. If you want to be beaten up, I volunteer to try.

TOM:

Jesus Christ, heebie, you couldn't do it alone. You're probably all vegetarians.

(*To* AJAX)

What did you do that for? You go two steps underneath and all your minds start falling apart. Have a drink?

JABEZ:

Someone give me a cigarette.

(IRIS *fumbles in her purse. She lights a cigarette for* JABEZ.)

ANNA:

My first husband was like this one. What a sonofabitch! He liked to see everyone squirm. I never could believe a word he said. The rotten bastard—he wanted to tie me up every time we went to bed.

TOM:

Bosslady! Give a woman a job and she grows balls. Hey! Come here! Is it true what they say about Chinese girls?

ANNA:

Ajax! We can't go on like this.

AJAX:

The whole thing is so out of fashion that I'm hypnotized. I don't believe he exists. He's an apparition. We should try to dissect him, humanely, of course. I'm no magician, I can't make him disappear. Tonight I wanted to do my giant-size hero. But then I'm here to protect everyone, including bigots. Unless you want me to leave. I think Mr. Stark gets the idea.

STARK:

(*Grunts*)

ANNA:

Don't think about going. We'll figure out something with this thing.

AJAX:

Why don't we both leave? We'll have a graduation ceremony, we'll play *Pomp and Circum* . . .

TOM:

Faggot! Faggot!

ANNA:

You can't leave now. And you can't ask me to leave after the show tonight. It isn't fair. It would imply a happy ending.

AJAX:

Not to me.

ANNA:

We'll not have a happy ending on my night. We will not have a sad ending. My night is the night of the paradoxical ending. Besides, I see no great transformation in you.

AJAX:

You wouldn't know what a transformation looked like because you look for big changes where there are only small ones.

TOM:

What a bunch of whores!

IRIS:

And what's wrong with whores!

JABEZ:

Do you want a punch in the mouth?

TOM:

(*Laughs*)

STARK:

(*Groans*)

ANNA:

Don't hit him. That's what he wants. Don't give him what he wants.

TOM:

Jesus Christ! What do you people do? I mean for a living?

AJAX:

You ask what you wouldn't answer. I don't mind telling you though. We are a group of investors and dealers. We deal in uranium stocks.

(*Enter* ACE *with a tray of sandwiches. Passes the tray around.*)

AJAX:

It's a simple scheme. It wouldn't cost you very much to buy into it. We could use you as a front man. Sure, I'll bet we could increase your investment threefold.

It's easy–all you need is a good pitch.

TOM:

You're nuts.

AJAX:

You're nuts if you don't take this opportunity. Secret power undreamed of. Jabez can show you. Jabez, show this man your pitch.

JABEZ:

(*Arranges the mannequin and himself*)
I operate on the suburban home. My palms always sweat on reaching the door. Clutching my leatherette briefcase, I ring the bell. The door opens.
(*Knees sag; looking in every direction he straightens up*)
Ohhh! I'm so glad you are home, my dear woman.
(*Begins mauling and gouging the mannequin*)
My name is Herman Gestalt. You know the house on Orchard Street that burned down? Mine. Yes, it was mine. Don't be alarmed. It wasn't too bad for me, but the children are in the hospital. Don't worry. It's only superficial burns. A glass of water? Please, I don't want to trouble you, just let me have a glass of water. You're a good-looking woman.
(*Sits*)
Thank you. Thank you.

(TOM *laughs.* JABEZ *transfers his attack to* TOM.)

I don't know how to begin. Yes, I do. I don't want charity. I wouldn't think of it. I'm too proud. I've got some very valuable securities. Uranium. Sssssh! Not a word. Uranium. Out West in Wyoming there are natural resources that would stagger the imagination.

(*Searching* TOM's *pockets*)

Oh, forgive me. I've been so busy trying to get the money for all the bills.

(*Showing the theatre stubs, etc., from* TOM's *pockets*)

I don't want to take up any more of your time. Look, just look at these. One hundred shares of Uranium, Unlimited. Send the kids to college. They're selling for two dollars a share now. But in a few . . .

(*Begins a hacking cough*)

Excuse me, the smoke is still in my lungs. The smoke. My mind isn't all here.

(*Takes* TOM's *handkerchief and starts crying. Holds up* TOM's *pocketwatch*)

This is fine. Thank you. Thank you.

(STARK *flays his arms imitative of* JABEZ.)

ANNA:

(*Using the mannequin*)

Take my money, take the furniture, repair the gutters, take, take, take. But please remove your twisted body from my sight. Get out! Get out!

TOM:

Where I come from they don't let animals like you run around loose. That Jewboy is all right though. He's trying to be comic. Hey, Steppin' Fetchit, bring something to drink!

(ACE *and* JABEZ *start to* TOM. AJAX *intercedes.*)

AJAX:

Wait one moment, gentlemen. There is only one man in this room capable of demolishing this piece of filth.

TOM:

And who is that, Mister Fu Man Chu?

AJAX:

(*Faces* MR. STARK *to* TOM)

Here he is.

TOM:

Get that creep away from me!

ACE:

I'm betting on Mr. Stark.

(*Throws a coin on the floor*)

AJAX:

Gee whiz, you're not backing out? I want this fight to be fair. Ace, you be the referee.

JABEZ:

This guy is going to kill my buddy Mr. Stark. I'll take up your bet, Ace.

(*Throws a handkerchief on the floor*)

AJAX:

Mr. Stark is the better man. Here's my bet.
(*Takes* JABEZ' *painting and throws it on the floor*)
It's all an artist can do—bet on his work.

IRIS:

Here's my contribution. You know the Bible. An arm for an arm.
(*Throws the mannequin's arm on the floor*)
You're getting just what—

ANNA:

I'd like to have it stick in your throat!
(*Throws the apple core on the floor*)

TOM:

Don't go too far. I've got a bad heart.

(*They crowd around* TOM *forcing him to face* MR. STARK. MR. STARK *advances and falls on* TOM. ACE *pulls them apart.* TOM, *gasping, staggers out into the audience and expires.* ACE, *while going to get him and dragging him back on stage, counts to ten slowly.*)

IRIS:

He's not moving.

ANNA:

Don't panic. Don't panic.
(*Examines* TOM)
Shit. He's not breathing. On my night, too.

ACE:

(*Puts his ear to* TOM's *chest*)

Dead as a dog.
(*Gently kicks* TOM)

JABEZ:
This is ridiculous.

ANNA:
Somebody will have to call the police.

IRIS:
He's not moving.

STARK:
(*A long groan*)

JABEZ:
Don't call the police. We'll have to refund everyone's money. That was a terrible thing to say. Yes, let's call the police.

AJAX:
Forget it. Let him stay there.

ANNA:
You said that as if you meant it. We can't let him just stay there.

AJAX:
Somebody in the audience will call the police.

ANNA:
You can't leave.

AJAX:
I'm not leaving. I'm going out to eat and put on some

make-up. I have to prepare myself for the police. (*Exits*)

JABEZ:

No one will believe this.

IRIS:

Why doesn't he move? He just couldn't die like this. If he's dead I'll get so mad he'll never forget it.

(ACE *collects the bet objects and exits.* ANNA, IRIS, *and* JABEZ *help* MR. STARK *exit. There is a slow crossfade of stage and house lights under the following:* TOM *begins to move. He finally stands and stares at the audience. He starts to say something when* ACE *interrupts him from the rear speaker.* TOM's *mouth keeps moving, but no sound comes forth. Near the end of* ACE's *speech* TOM *begins mouthing* ACE's *words.*)

ACE:

It's cold. It's cold. Like January one in the temperate zones. Look at him showing you his credentials. Ha. Ha. As if he still had to prove that he had that thing called identity. You need more than that piece of paper. Anyone call the police? Never mind. Look at the person next to you. Go ahead! We're all here together. Do you think they have some kind of communicable disease? I mean will it be a fatal look? Do you think death can be caught like the common cold? Take your mind off it. After this intermission, the breather, we plan a life behind the senses. Ooo-oh, look at the man saying, "I'm not dead. Can't you hear me? Can't you see I'm alive? Are you deaf and blind? I'm not dead."

(TOM *disappears.*)

Well, it's his illusion.

(*Stage dark.*)

He doesn't know he's dead yet. We will see who is and who ain't dead.

Act Two

Players are arranged in a tableau around TOM. IRIS *begins humming.* TOM *begins moving and stands up.*

TOM:

What is this?

ACE:

You are dead.

TOM:

I am not.

ACE:

You'll realize that you are dead in three or four days. The quicker you accept it the better off you will be.

ANNA:

(*Laughs*)

Don't be so serious. We forgive you. It isn't terrifying yet. Everyone goes through the judgement.

TOM:

I want to get out of this.

ACE:

How?

TOM:

Can't I start a fight? If I had money I could get out of it.

ACE:

(*Putting his arm on the table*)

Want to arm wrestle?

TOM:

Not with you.

ACE:

It's all over. I've judged you.

TOM:

That quick?

(*Blackout.*)

TOM:

It can't be that quick. I didn't do anything. Turn on the lights. I want light. I want the day to start over again.

(*Lights up.* AJAX *and* ANNA *are working behind a counter. He cleans his side of the counter and she cleans her half.*)

ANNA:

You don't look like a counterman. You don't talk like a counterman. I'll bet you took this job for kicks. You probably have a rich father. And you took this job to show him you could make good on your own.

(*Enter* TOM.)

TOM:

Coffee.

ANNA:

Draw one!

TOM:

And toast.

ANNA:

Side of toast!

(*Gives* TOM *a glass of water*)

Did you go out last night? Who'd you go out with? I bet you went out with Geraldine. You got such lousy taste in women. They're old enough to be your mother. Yeah, you're a real case all right. Hasn't that Geraldine cost you enough? That's why you ain't the manager. Sure it is. You could have been the manager. What a lousy business we're doing this morning. Hey, look, a funeral. I wonder who it is. If there is one thing that really bothers me it's not knowing who that is that they're burying. Who is it? It could be Geraldine and you wouldn't care. Not you. You know it could be my own mother and I wouldn't know. My mother wasn't too well the last time I saw her.

TOM:

What's the name of this town?

ANNA:

[Gives name of town]

TOM:

You're wrong.

(*Pulls out a gun and shoots* ANNA)

(*Blackout.* JABEZ *and* IRIS *are seated at a table.* MR. STARK *is on all fours beside the table.* TOM *enters and circles the table.*)

JABEZ:

Where's the coffee?

IRIS:

I forgot to buy coffee.

JABEZ:

Forgot? Forgot? You don't forget to dress or to take two hours every morning to make up. To hell with that! That's no excuse.

(TOM *kicks* MR. STARK.)

STARK:

(*Groans*)

IRIS:

Did you walk the dog this morning?

JABEZ:

No, I didn't walk the dog this morning. I never wanted the thing in the first place. Now, all of a sudden, I'm the keeper of the dog.

IRIS:

I only asked. Besides, you know you love that dog more than anything else in the world.

JABEZ:

I hate your sweetness. It's so damn false.

(JABEZ *raises his hand mockingly and strikes* TOM. TOM *kicks* MR. STARK.)

JABEZ:

You're not worth hitting. Do you see what happens when I don't have coffee?

STARK:

(*Groans*)

IRIS:

Oh, can't you see the dog is suffering? Take him out. Poor baby!

JABEZ:

Come to your papa, big doggie.
(*Pats* MR. STARK)
You're not hurt are you? Hey, boy, you forgive me, don't you?

IRIS:

The dog is female.

JABEZ:

You idiot! You and your manners! Phooey! Phoney bitch!

STARK:

(*Groans*)

IRIS:

Quit being irrational and take the dog for a walk. Poor baby.

JABEZ:

Will you stop treating that animal as if he were a child? It's just a dog.

IRIS:

If you could give me a child I wouldn't mother the dog. The dog is female.

JABEZ:

If you had just two ideas in that head of yours you could marry them off and have all the children you wanted.

(TOM *puts his hands around* IRIS' *throat.*)

STARK:

(*Groans*)

JABEZ:

I'll take you out now, boy. That should shut you up.

(*Blackout.* TOM *and* AJAX *are sitting at a table. On the table is an insect mask.* AJAX *has his arm in a sling.*)

TOM:

(*Unable to look at* AJAX *and rubbing his wrists*)
Does it get worse?
(*Pause*)
You're not very different from myself. Our spirits are the same. Does it get worse?
(*Pause*)
It's almost like working in the old silent comedies. You would have been great.
(*Pause*)
Well, it really doesn't cut working in those days. The bite is gummy. Too much talk. You . . . you . . . you won't betray–

AJAX:

(*Puts on the insect mask and screams*)

I'll release you if you kiss me.

(TOM *exits.*)

AJAX:

As a master of judo, jujitsu and karate, heed my words.

(*Limps around*)

Give up your homes which are not much anyway as you very well know. Give up your children and your nagging spouses. Come with me beyond the marked trails to a life of simplicity. I will teach you to take care of yourself.

(*Strikes the mannequin*)

Look around you! Two pig faces are rubbing noses. Each hoping their time-bomb hearts won't explode. So what if they don't explode? Some Arab, or Jew, or Chink, or if you like irony an Indian, will trip the lever. I am the master. I could break a brick in two . . . I could demonstrate every twist and turn known to the secret of judo players. . . . Don't let this mask fool you! I am the master. I am not trying to hide anything. There is good reason to wear this mask.

(*Raises mask*)

I was in Mexico when I chanced upon a greasy restaurant. The rest should be obvious. Chili peppers. That curse of mankind! The heat from one chili pepper equals that of a hydrogen bomb.

(*Screams*)

Don't worry. It only attacks every seven minutes. The master's face will regain its natural color in a few days. Eat, sleep, and work. What else do you have? Oh, yes, an occasional rape or beating. And then what do you do? Run, run for the police crying against the fates. Bah! Come along with me where I can show you how a real defense is made.

(*Lights fading. Lowers mask.*)

Come along to a pastoral life. Come along. Be careful of the one next to you. He has murder in his heart. Come along. Come along.

(*Blackout.* TOM *is seated at a table.* ANNA *is stroking his hair.* JABEZ *chases* IRIS *across the stage.*)

TOM:

Boy! Boy! Bring me more to drink!

(ACE *enters with a tray.*)

Drink it!

(ACE *drinks.*)

(*To* ANNA)

And you drink it, too!

(ANNA *drinks.*)

Good. Now I'll drink. Go away, boy, until I call for more.

(ACE *exits.*)

(*To* ANNA)

Kiss me!

(ANNA *kisses* TOM.)

Where's my son? Where's my son? Come here immediately!

(*Enter* MR. STARK.)

Where have you been? What have you learned today?

(*Strikes* MR. STARK)

Do you want a woman?

(*Laughs*)

Get out! Get out!

(MR. STARK *exits.*)

(*To* ANNA)

Kiss me!

(ANNA *kisses* TOM.)

Where's my money maker? Where's my money maker?

(*Takes a small black mustache from a black bag and puts it on*)

(JABEZ *enters.*)

Don't fawn over me! I know you're plotting against me! I know everything! Don't bother to lie! Just remember I'm watching you at all times. Get out! Get out!

(JABEZ *exits.*)

(*To* ANNA)

Kiss me!

(ANNA *kisses* TOM.)

Where's my second in command? Where's my . . .

(AJAX *enters wearing a mustache that insists on falling off. He puts another mustache on* ANNA.)

I know you are plotting against me. Don't bother to lie! I've had my eye on you. Remember: all is war. Get out! Get out!

(AJAX *exits.* ANNA *kisses* TOM. JABEZ *chases* IRIS *across the stage.*)

Did I ask you to kiss me? Never mind, everything I need to know is in here.

(*Points to his black bag*)

(ANNA *puts on an ant mask.*)

What do you want from me? You'll get nothing out of me. Where is my second wife? Where is my second wife? Get out! Get out!

(*Exit* ANNA. *Enter* IRIS *wearing a butterfly mask.*)

Oh, my true loved one. Come to me. Come to me.

(*Puts his hands around* IRIS' *waist, but can't kiss her*)

You're all alike! Tramps! Treacherous tramps!

IRIS:

You should walk the dog. He hasn't been out in days!

TOM:

Get out! Get out!

(IRIS *exits.*)

How can I do it? How can it be done? There must be a way.

(*Takes a mirror and several articles of black clothing from the bag; puts the clothes on*)

You must have faith. You must. Am I not the one who can foresee real peace? Yes, I am the one. I see harmony where others only see chaos. I will banish sickness. The people will listen to me. They will listen. But what can you say to the stupid peasants? What? They have no minds. They are impossible. Fear is the only answer. They don't understand anything but that.

(JABEZ *with a fox mask chases* IRIS *across the stage.* AJAX *and* ANNA *enter with* MR. STARK, *wearing a dog mask, in a baby stroller.*)

Get out! Get out!

(JABEZ *catches* IRIS *and kisses her.*)

Get out! Get out! Boy! Boy! Bring me something to drink! They are at it again. I can't trust anyone. Fools! Fools! I bring the secrets of happiness.

(TOM *sits.* ACE *enters wearing a tiger mask and pours a bottle of wine over* TOM. TOM *is in ecstasy. Heavy knocking on the door.*)

I knew they were coming for me. Fools!

(*Pounding on the door as the lights fade to a blackout. More pounding on the door in the dark. Lights up.* AJAX *is in* TOM'*s place.* TOM *enters in an S.S. uniform.*)

TOM:

So what kind of gathering do we have here? You can't hide from me. You are all under arrest. Don't you understand? You are all under arrest.

IRIS:

I thought I sent you out to walk the dog.

(*Hums "Stars and Stripes Forever"*)

TOM:

This place is surrounded by my faithful body servants.

AJAX:

Go away. You are boring us.

TOM:

Don't you understand? I am arresting you for your own good. I do the deed and I take the guilt. For example, take your mangled child. I'll kill him and you can be free.

STARK:

(*Groans*)

TOM:

And your women. When you're tired of your women, I'll give you others and I'll take care of them. And that goes for procuring men, too. You can have anything. I'll die for you. Again and again, I'll die. What more can you ask of me?

ANNA:

(*Confidentially. To* TOM)
He doesn't look like a counterman. I'll bet he's only taken this job to prove to his rich father that he can make it on his own.

AJAX:

He's a false prophet.

TOM:

I know what I'm doing. Don't worry about that. I

know. That's what you would like, yes, you would like to know. Well, I'll tell you when the time comes. When the time comes I'll let you know.

JABEZ:

What do you think you're in? A dream? This is no dream.

TOM:

You don't have to remind me of that! I'll take care of your insolence!
(*Shoots* JABEZ, *but* JABEZ *is unmoved*)

ACE:

I'm hungry and there's nothing in the kitchen. I just wonder how tender this cat will be after I broil him.
(*The cast closes in around* TOM. *Lights fade.* TOM *starts shooting.*)

TOM:

Change the scene! Please, God, change this scene! Hurry, hurry up!
(*Blackout. Lights up on* ANNA *on one side of stage.*)

ANNA:

Come over to our side. You're not doing anything important. What do you do all day? Read the papers? You have a job! And you vote! You really make up your own mind? You don't know who you are until you're dead. Wouldn't you like to know? Life is so apathetic! Everything in your life changes from day to day.

(*Lights up on* ACE *on the other side of stage.*)

ACE:

To hell with life! Ain't nothing going to ever change there. Same old story. Black and white and white and black. Always everyone is fighting.

ANNA:

Isn't it confusing and then just boring? Life is such a bore! Come over to our side. We've got some absolute values you've never heard about.

ACE:

The reformers never reform. Don't tell me you are still hung up on that freedom bullshit? You don't know what freedom is until you feel the yoke.

ANNA:

Oh, I don't want you to do anything right now. Just remember all your friends are doing it. Don't act hastily. Think about it. And don't worry about the family. Bring the kids along. It's like getting married all over again. This time forever.

ACE:

You want me to be the same all the time. But change is my nature. You'll get your taste. You ever watch a stew cooking on a stove? The meat juices are just cooking and trickling in the vegetable juices and everything is changing and cooking.

(*Blackout. The mannequin is on the table.* JABEZ *and* MR. STARK *are over it.*)

JABEZ:

I don't care what anyone says. To me, you are a buddha. Hand me the glue.

(*Takes the glue from* MR. STARK *and starts gluing the arms to the mannequin*)

Really, I mean it. You don't want anything. That's the key. You can't fall down if you don't want anything.

STARK:

(*Grunts*)

JABEZ:

I've always wanted to be a doctor. Fix up the natives. Ah, to be adored for my good nature. From afar, that is. I want everything.

STARK:

(*Grunts*)

JABEZ:

Oh, I envy you. No. No. You are not a freak. I'm a freak, but not you. In my native village you are next to God. Much higher than I am. It's just because I have to put up this front of meanness. You know the old cantankerous doc.

STARK:

(*Grunts*)

JABEZ:

And most of all, I must be indecipherable. Like you, in a way. Only with venom.
(*Grunts*)
See? Like that. Everywhere I go it's just like that. Now don't you feel like a buddha?

STARK:

(*Grunts*)

(*Enter* IRIS.)

JABEZ:

Ah, here comes the nurse.

IRIS:

I'm not your nurse.

JABEZ:

I think we've made an important scientific discovery, nurse. Here in the deepest recesses of the jungle, we have discovered the secret of life. It will be tough to prove it to the world, but we have the living proof right here.
(*Points to the mannequin*)

IRIS:

You're always goofing around with dead things. Don't I count? Don't you want me? Don't you want me?

JABEZ:

Doesn't everyone want you?

IRIS:

You're a paranoid!

JABEZ:

You're a whore! No, not that, you are not a whore!

IRIS:

I'm whatever you want me to be. Don't torture yourself! I'm your apple, baby.

JABEZ:

And I'm your snake doctor.
(*Embraces* IRIS)
Cover that native's eyes!

(*Enter* TOM.)

TOM:

Stop this nonsense. Stop it!

JABEZ:

What language are you speaking?

IRIS:

He's a funny looking native. I've never seen one like him before.

TOM:

Stop it. Can't I make you understand that kissing will only lead to babies.

STARK:

(*Baby moans*)

TOM:

I can't stand the sight of copulating couples.

(ACE *wheels in the baby carriage with* AJAX *and* ANNA *in it.*)

ACE:

Doctor! Doctor! Two of my villagers are stuck together!

TOM:

I can't bear this any longer. I want to go back to living.
(*Collapses*)

JABEZ:

(*To* ACE)
You take care of the magic. I'll take care of the humanity.

STARK:

(*A long baby groan*)

(*Lights fade out.*)

Act Three

Players are arranged in tableau as in the beginning of Act Two, except TOM *and* ACE *are missing.*

AJAX:

The interesting thing is Watson, we know the gentleman isn't dead. Therefore, let us proceed without the body. We don't need the body. Start singing, Iris.

IRIS:

Don't give me any orders! This is your responsibility, Anna.

AJAX:

We don't need the body. Many rituals are performed without it.

ANNA:

Where the hell is Ace? And the dead one. You just can't trust a lush.

JABEZ:

I've seen the guy somewhere. I swear I have. Where was it?

IRIS:

He did look familiar, honey. Don't bother your head. You aren't supposed to remember everything. Artists . . .

ANNA:

They can't do this to us. Why did he have to come here the night I'm running things?

JABEZ:

I know. Now I know! I don't know his name, but I know where I've seen him. I remember he was in a film with Charlie Chaplin. Yes, yes. He stood in the background of a prison scene. Somehow they had Charlie in prison and he was one of the inmates. He didn't do anything. He just stood there.

(*From the rear speaker the noises of a fight are heard.*)

TOM:

(*From rear*)
Frauds! Frauds!

ACE:

(*From rear*)
Calm down, you sonofabitch! Get a sedative! Someone get a sedative!

TOM:

Leave me alone. I'm all right. Get your hands off me. Nigger! Yeooooow!

ACE:

The switch is on. Turn that thing . . .

(*Long pause.* ACE *enters.*)

AJAX:

Can anything be done? Well, it looks like we'll just have to do without the body after all.

(JABEZ *starts to leave.*)

ANNA:

No! If one goes then everyone will want to go. We'll start something else.

ACE:

I could cook up some kind of fake African dance. It's been known to make the body come back.

(ACE *kicks up one leg lazily.* JABEZ *begins a chant.* AJAX *bangs on the table.* MR. STARK *joins in with moaning.*)

I didn't ask for tom-toms.

ANNA:

I don't want a mood piece! I'm tired of satires on the race issue. And I'm tired of satires on satires.

ACE:

Bosslady, you can afford to say that.

JABEZ:

I'm going back to soap opera.

AJAX:

What do you want? A problem play—with death being the problem?

STARK:

(*Grunts*)

IRIS:

(*To* AJAX)

You give me a pain.

JABEZ:

Pain? Pain? You don't know anything about pain!

I've got pains you've never conceived of. This place is a pressure machine. It's a band of steel around the temples applied like a medieval tourniquet. The pressure on the head becomes so great that the pain passes from it. It rushes down the spine. Everywhere there is pain and then I want to faint and there is no pain, nothing, a void. You don't give me a pain, my dear hustling wife. You are pain.

(*Wild laughter off stage.* IRIS *hums nervously.* ACE *exits.*)

Can't you hear the pain?

AJAX:

Help! Help! I'm trapped in a Chinese restaurant!

ANNA:

That's not very funny.

AJAX:

Oh, baby, I didn't want to hurt your feelings. I'm a thoughtless rotten creature. My tongue doesn't belong to me.

(*Holds* ANNA)

ANNA:

I know all about your tongue.

AJAX:

That's unfair! You sweet, lovely Oriental bitch!

ANNA:

I know about your hands, too!

AJAX:

Where is your Oriental calmness?

ANNA:

You sonofabitch! You can afford to bait me. You haven't anything to lose. You can always fall back on your rich father.

AJAX:

That's your fantasy! I can no more go back to my father than you to a hand laundry. Oh, my tongue again! Forgive it!

ANNA:

You are more of an Oriental than I am.

STARK:

(*Groans*)

JABEZ:

(*To* IRIS)

Why can't you have dignity like that?

(AJAX *puts his hands between* ANNA's *legs. She slaps him.*)

IRIS:

Dignity? Rich fathers? Falling back? Tune in tomorrow. Will Anna, daughter of the rich and famous egg roll manufacturer, keep her dignity? Masquerading as a coolie hipster, she is trying to have the world accept her for herself and not her good looks, money, or charm. Will Ajax, son of rich father type 37B, pull himself together, marry her and . . . I like marriage as an end. It tells us that we have witnessed a comedy. (*Backstage noise of breaking glass.*)

Please don't say anything. Marriage is the end. No comments about the relationships between men and women are necessary.

AJAX:

That's my name. Mr. Relationship. Don't I look like a relationship? Don't answer! As Mr. Relationship I give the commands. Jabez! Tell us about your end.

JABEZ:

To tell the truth, Mr. Relationship, the only reason I keep you around is to solve my problems.

IRIS:

Can't you ever stop using clichés?

JABEZ:

Now my biggest problem is my throat. I want to stop smoking. But I also am an actor. On the surface there doesn't seem to be any conflict. But what happens? I'm always getting roles where I have to be a chain smoker on stage. Is that fair? I ask you.

AJAX:

How would I know? I'm only a relationship!

JABEZ:

Oh, you mean I'm getting what I deserve.

AJAX:

You said it, I didn't.

TOM:

(*From backstage*)
It won't work! Warden! Warden!

JABEZ:

(*Painting*)
Sure. Well, there's work. Man needs work and he needs a relationship to it. That's all that counts. Be a doctor and go into the jungle and heal the savages whether they like it or not. Or be a teacher and teach the illiterates of the world. Build bridges. There's a lot of work to be done. Collect money for all the hungry poeples of the world. I swear it gives me a coronary to just think of it. Bullshit! I heard that out there! What did you expect? Love?

AJAX:

I don't have any values. Man, you have to supply them. I'm only a go-between.

JABEZ:

Sure, I know. I'll be a musician. Blow words on the wind. Pay no attention to what's happening around me. Use it, use what is around you, but don't stop to say hello. Don't get dragged down. Fly, soar, slap paint, color it, keep going, keep your eye on the vision. If your wings get clipped, grow new ones.

(*Backstage noise.*)

TOM:

(*From backstage*)
Leave me alone! Don't! Leave me alone!

JABEZ:

If you have a woman make her dedicated. Believe me, it won't work otherwise. She'll bake bread, have children, sweep your wooden floors, and mend your clothes. If she won't do any of these things make sure she does have something "creative" to do. Any kind of performing will do. And she definitely is not to wear make-up. Maybe a little eye shadow. But, damn it, cut her hair short. In a few years she'll be like any other fine male companion.

AJAX:

You can go around knocking the basic stuff of life. That's your business. Don't blame me. I could enrich your life.

(*Backstage noise.*)

TOM:

(*From backstage*)
I can't! Go on!

ANNA:

In the beginning the woman ate beans and had children. Now the woman is either a cook or a dyke. I don't like your categories.

AJAX:

Okay, I'm convinced. It's very dull being Mr. Relationship.

STARK:

(*A long groan*)

ANNA:

I'm what you want me to be!

(*Wild laughter off stage. It stops as* TOM *enters with* ACE *following him.* TOM *examines everyone. He sits.*)

ANNA:

A long time ago I was married to a drummer named Cookie. We made all the goddamn sessions. One night after a session, a bunch of us went to another drummer's place. After awhile there were only three of us left. I was beautifully tired. The sun shot around the window shades and you could see the motes floating. Somehow the other drummer started putting Cookie's playing down. He said some terrible things, some true and some not true at all. Then the drummer started putting me down. It became worse and worse. He asked me to take off my fucking clothes We got up to leave. He bolted the door and pulled out a knife. I feel the same way now.

(TOM *shows his empty hands, makes stiff dance gestures, and laughs.*)

AJAX:

What happened?

ANNA:

Nothing. Nothing ever happens. Cookie talked and talked and talked. Finally the drummer invited us to eat breakfast with him and to sleep over. We just had to get out of there.

AJAX:

Did you ever see him again?

ANNA:

Sure, many times.

TOM:

(*To* IRIS)

And now would you step into the office. I'll look at your teeth.

(*Pause.*)

JABEZ:

I'm ready.

TOM:

Very well then.

(JABEZ *sits in a chair and opens his mouth.*)

Lovely, lovely. But I suppose you con men must keep up appearances. Do I or do I not have a nurse?

IRIS:

What do you want?

TOM:

More blood for my experiments. Shut up and get to work! We have an important extraction at hand.

AIRIS *hands* TOM *paper tools as in Act One.* TOM *examines the tools and discards them one by one. He uses his hands to explore* JABEZ' *mouth.)*

ANNA:

(To audience)

So many times one comes to an experience not knowing what will happen next. I think it's important to tell you what I think will happen. In that way I hope you will give up searching for clues to a climax that doesn't exist.

AJAX:

You can't have a climax without a series of small wars.

ANNA:

Or if it does exist it is less important than the people involved.

(TOM *begins to pull out of* JABEZ' *mouth an American flag, a Confederate flag, a Russian flag, an Israeli flag, a city flag, etc., muttering the name of the flag and his total rejection of it with "Bah!" or "Ugh!")*

Nothing is going to happen.

(TOM *pulls a half-eaten apple out of* JABEZ' *mouth.)*

TOM:

Will you shut up! I'm getting close.

ANNA:

The nature of nothing . . .

(TOM *throws the rotten apple at the mannequin.* ANNA *sits.)*

TOM:

This is a madhouse.

AJAX:

Do you know what a vasectomy is? It's a small, neat piece of surgery. The seminal vessels are knotted and the sperm can never find their way out. It happened about the same time you were threatened by a nameless drummer.

ANNA:

I know.

(TOM *rips an arm off the mannequin.*)

AJAX:

(*To* TOM)

Shut up and sit down!

(*To* ANNA)

What do you mean, you know?

ANNA:

I just know, that's all. You're my man.

AJAX:

Oh yeah, for how long?

ANNA:

Don't start that again, please.

(TOM *starts dancing with the mannequin.*)

STARK:

(*Groans*)

ACE:

That man don't eat right. It's all in the food you eat. Believe me, if you would just feed the world properly there'd be no war, no hate, no insanity. Take that man. He probably doesn't eat breakfast. If I fed him for a few months he'd be a happy man. Oh, he'd have his same old problems. But the difference would be in his approach. I'm telling you, it's all in the body chemistry. You got to give the body vitamins, proteins, enzymes, you got to keep up the sugar level in your brain, you . . . I don't want to get too technical. You get my meaning.

TOM:

You have exquisite movements, my dear. They're talking about us. We don't care. Let them talk. What did you say you did? An airline hostess? How perfectly charming. Oh, my dear, I'm not that old.

JABEZ:

Aren't you an old-time movie actor?

TOM:

I hear them. I hear them. They're not actors. No precision. No ideas, not like the old days. No, my dear, I'm not old enough to be your father. It's getting stuffy in here. Oh, I love the way you glide.

JABEZ:

That man needs help, but I don't think he can eat his way out of this one.

TOM:

Oh my, they simply will not leave us alone. Let's sit this one out. I said let's sit this one out. Didn't you hear me? My legs are getting tired. Dear girl, I am not an airplane. This must stop. I mean it. Stop dancing! You little cunt! Stop!

(*Throws the mannequin on the floor and kicks it. Lifts the imaginary clothing on the body*)

Oh, I'm dreadfully sorry. You are a man.

(*Runs into the audience and back*)

You're trying to mix me up!

(TOM *lunges toward* ANNA, *but* MR. STARK, *no longer acting the spastic, intervenes.*)

STARK:

(*Holding* TOM)

Somebody call an ambulance! This is ridiculous!

TOM:

He speaks! A miracle! I've performed a miracle! He speaks! I made it happen! I am cause. I'm Christ . . .

STARK:

Sssshhh! It's all right. I'm going to let you go. And you are going to take it easy. Ace, watch him.

(ACE *sits* TOM *down.* STARK *begins to exit.*)

TOM:

Don't leave! You're my disciple.

(STARK *stops.*)

ANNA:

Damn it, Ajax! You never stop kidding! Who the hell are you?

STARK:

An actor. [States his name and phone number]

ANNA:

Oh, I get it.

JABEZ:

Well I don't get anything.

IRIS:

But why did you want to play a spastic?

STARK:

You've never wanted to play a spastic? It was an incredible opportunity.

AJAX:

I say the fellow is a rogue!

STARK:

(*Exiting*)

I'm not the joker here.

TOM:

Get out of here! Creep, get out!

(ANNA *moves to* TOM. AJAX *stops her.*)

AJAX:

There's no talking to him, Anna. He's much beyond that.

TOM:

(*Grabs a mannequin arm and begins swinging it slowly and then wildly*)
It doesn't pay to be lyrical like you. It isn't worth it. Can't you leave an old man alone? Where's your respect? You believe too much of what you read. You believe too much.
(*Starts to audience, but stops*)

ACE:

(*To* TOM)
Are you all right?

TOM:

Yes, I'm terribly sorry.
(*Sits down*)
Really, I don't know what got into me. I'm all right. I don't usually get this excited.

IRIS:

I don't like it. But I guess we'll just have to put him away.

ANNA:

What can we do?

IRIS:

Maybe we can send him back where he came from. Find out where he comes from. What is your name?

TOM:

Oscar Wilde! What the hell is it to you?

ACE:

Calm down. Don't fret. Don't despair. You be a good fellow and I'll fix you a meal like you never ate before. Seaweed, mustard greens, butterfish . . .

IRIS:

That's what comes of sharing taxis.

TOM:

(*Starts juggling imaginary balls*)
I knew you were here. You're on my radio. It wasn't what I expected. I wanted to do slapstick. Intelligent slapstick. I wanted . . . I wanted to perform again. I had something in mind.

(AJAX *begins singing "Remember Pearl Harbor."*)

ANNA:

Stop baiting him!

AJAX:

Why should I treat him any differently than anyone else? I don't get any special treatment because I'm insane.

TOM:

He's absolutely correct.

ACE:

(*To* TOM)
Yes, general. The attack has subsided, general.

TOM:

(*Breaks something and screams*)

Shut up!
(*Dashes for* IRIS; JABEZ, ACE *and* AJAX *fight him into a chair*)

IRIS:

I'll bet he got that way in the war. The poor de . . .
(STARK *enters.*)

STARK:

They won't come.

JABEZ:

What do you mean, they won't come?

STARK:

Exactly that. That's what I was told over the phone. They won't come and get him. They said he had to turn himself in.

ANNA:

That's all I needed.

TOM:

(*Jumps up with a weapon like a stick or something lying around*)
You can't fool me. I'm not going anywhere. I'm just starting.
(*Jumps into the audience*)
I'm just starting. Where's Abe Lincoln? I'm just starting to find out what this is all about. I'm going places, but you're not sending me anywhere.
(*Fakes a few passes with his weapon at the audience*

and laughs)
You know what I think? Wait a minute. Don't move
—anybody.
(*Long pause*)
Don't worry about me. Worry about yourself.
(*Laughs a long time and returns to stage*)

IRIS:
I thought he was going to say something I hadn't heard before.

JABEZ:
You would think that.

IRIS:
Let's go! Come on, let's go! We've got to take him. If they won't come here, we'll just have to take him there.

JABEZ:
I can't do it. I don't care what you think. I can't do it. Have you ever been inside one of those places? You can do it. Not me. Inside or out, I don't know which is worse. I won't try to stop you.

AJAX:
(*To* TOM)
What do you want to do?

TOM:
I don't know. It's nice here now. I don't want to hurt anyone. I should turn myself in. It would be the best

thing. I guess so.

STARK:

I'm so glad you said that. It'll be all right. Don't worry.

TOM:

Don't touch me!

(TOM *jumps up. He grabs the mannequin and begins growling. He tries putting the mannequin together again. When unsuccessful,* TOM *rips the arm off again. He bangs its head.* IRIS *approaches. He growls.*)

ANNA:

Will somebody do something?

AJAX:

Why try to do anything?

ANNA:

Because there are people watching us.

ACE:

Get back, Iris. Here, pooch! Come here, boy! Come on! I got a nice bone for you. Your master's voice is calling. Come on, pooch. Come on.

(TOM *crawls up toward* ACE. *He collapses.* STARK *picks him up.*)

TOM:

Leave me alone!

(*Breaks away*)

I know all of you.

(*The following incoherently*)
(*To* AJAX)
You can't stand being loved.
(*To Anna*)
Wanting to be loved.
(*Laughs. To* JABEZ)
Tomorrow.
(*Does a foot shuffle*)
(*To* IRIS)
You bite your fingernails.
(*To* STARK)
You'll do anything! You sonofabitch! Anything!
(*To* ACE)
And you, you . . .

(TOM *kicks the air trying to break something.* STARK *grabs him.*)

STARK:

Enough, enough. Who will help me get him to a hospital? I said, who . . . I'll do it myself.

AJAX:

I'll get a cab.
(*To audience*)
Don't look for me here tomorrow.
(*Exits*)

ANNA:

I'll go with you.

STARK:

He might get violent. We'll come back.

(ANNA *exits.*)

Ace, are you going to help me?

ACE:

Are you kidding? Well, I'll call the dog catcher. That's about the extent of it.

(STARK *exits with* TOM.)

IRIS:

Why don't you two guys get out of here. I'd like to take on this entire audience by myself.

JABEZ:

You want me to collect the money? Or are you doing this for kicks?

IRIS:

Long before I met you I took on a whole town.

ACE:

That's a lot of work, baby.

JABEZ:

You shut up!

ACE:

Woowee! My lips are sealed.

JABEZ:

What I don't understand is . . . Why won't you see me any place but on stage? You come late on purpose. I can't talk to you here. I can't make love to you here. I know, I know, it's the safest place in the world for you. Nothing can happen.

IRIS:

I wonder what will happen to that man?

JABEZ:

What do I care? They'll give him electric shock treatments or something like that. So what? I still have my problems.

IRIS:

Why wouldn't you go with the rest?

JABEZ:

Because no matter what happened I'd feel . . . Because I didn't think he . . . Because someone else . . . I don't know why, that's why.

IRIS:

I know why. In the back of that diabolical mind of yours there is a little lingering thought. If I stay, perhaps, maybe, if only the accidental word or gesture would start something real between us. Oh, it would be a play about Jabez and Iris. And if it did, if it did, you would be able to say the things you could never say and hear the things you could never hear and all the . . .

JABEZ:

Let's get out of here. Now.

(*Exit* JABEZ *and* IRIS.)

ACE:

(Straightens and cleans up)

It don't always work itself out this way. Well, let me take that back. In a way it does. I mean we don't have a madman every night. I don't like that guy. I know I'm supposed to feel for him, but I don't. Some of us will be back tomorrow. Some of us won't. You know, something dies and something is born. A little of the old faces and a few of the new. It could be you up here. There's only one ingredient necessary. You got to want. I don't care if you want a meal or if you come to steal. It'll work itself out. One way or the other. Look at this apple.

(To himself)

Close the show like a trouper, Ace.

(ANNA *enters, sits down and puts her face in her hands.*)

You can tell a lot of people wanted this apple because it's all chewed up. It's a good thing. I'm doing the talking because if Ajax were here he'd break in and tell you that this apple is a golden Chinese apple and stands for knowledge.

(*To* ANNA)

What's happening?

ANNA:

I hereby condemn you to inherit this place and all it contains. Ajax said he'd come back for me.

ACE:

Jabez and Iris?

ANNA:

When I saw them they were still fighting.

ACE:

That leaves Stark and the madman. Stark would turn into an apple for you. And the madman would throw the apple at you. Well, it's time to close up. Now don't come back without wanting something. Hear me? Okay. Okay.

(*Blackout.*)

END